360 COACH

A Biblical Approach to Coaching the Heart, Mind, and Body

BroadStreet
PUBLISHING

BroadStreet Publishing Group, LLC.
Savage, Minnesota, USA
Broadstreetpublishing.com

360 Coach © 2022 by Fellowship of Christian Athletes

978-1-4245-6552-8
978-1-4245-6553-5 (eBook)

FCA Editorial Team: Jordyn Hayden, Shea Vailes
FCA Writing Team: Mark Hull, Daniel Chappell, Kellen Cox, Kerry O'Neill

Design and typesetting by Garborg Design Works | garborgdesign.com
Additional editorial services by Michelle Winger | literallyprecise.com

Printed in China.

360
COACH

TABLE OF
CONTENTS

How to Use the 360 Coach Bible Study

Coach, welcome to a journey designed to strengthen your relationship with Jesus, affirm the significant role you have as a coach, and restore the beauty of sport under the rule and reign of King Jesus. This study is designed to grow you as a disciple of Jesus, give you a new purpose for coaching, and, in turn, empower you to impact the coaches and athletes around you.

We suggest you plan 30 minutes to one hour for each lesson. Each lesson contains the following segments:

PRE-GAME

Each lesson begins with a reminder to log in and watch the 360 Coach videos.

GAME TIME

This segment explores the biblical truths and how they apply to your life as a coach.

POST-GAME

Take time to review the questions, reflect on how the biblical truth applies to your life, and pray to close out your time.

Also featured throughout each segment are interactive opportunities to enhance your individual, Coaches Huddle, or 1-on-1 studies.

TALK ABOUT IT

Poignant questions written here will help individual reflection and group discussion.

360 COACHING POINT

Here you will find a key coaching point to take away from each lesson.

In the corresponding 360 Coach course, you will be joining a global community of coaches who also desire to live out the Kingdom of God in every area of their lives.

We want to help you become whole and complete in Christ, lacking nothing, so you can help your athletes become whole and complete as well.

 Visit 360coach.fca.org or scan the QR code to get started today!

Introduction

PRE-GAME

Log in to your 360 Coach account and watch the videos for this lesson.

GAME TIME

> After John was arrested, Jesus went to Galilee, proclaiming the good news of God: 'The time is fulfilled, and the kingdom of God has come near. Repent and believe the good news!' —Mark 1:14-15

Jesus begins His ministry with this stunning announcement: There's a new Kingdom and a new King. This is a Kingdom that functions in a vastly different way than all other kingdoms. And this is good news!

Over the next three years, Jesus' singular focus was to explain life in this Kingdom through His teachings and enact it through His miracles, compassion, and forgiveness of sins. In light of this announcement, Jesus is telling everyone to repent, to rethink everything, then believe and arrange their lives and actions around this new reality.

Assuming that sport has a place in God's Kingdom when Jesus returns to fully institute His Kingship, the questions below can help us rethink what sports should look like with a distinctly Christian worldview.

Take some time to discuss as a group.

TALK ABOUT IT

1. If Jesus became the governing authority over our sports programs, what things would He judge as perfectly acceptable to continue doing as we already are?

2. What would Jesus say are acceptable end results to strive for? How could we rethink our approach toward achieving those ends?

3. What things would Jesus say we need to completely abolish from programs because they do not line up with His values and have no future in His Kingdom?

If we are going to submit to Jesus in the environment of sport, we must rethink our approach to the central organizing principle of sport—competition. The two different approaches to competition can be summed up by these two words:

With and **Against**. When you think of competing, do you think about doing it with the other individual or team, or are you doing it against them?

This suggested warning label for competition was given in the third video:

WARNING: COMPETITION AS AN EXERCISE IN SELF-INTEREST CAN LEAD TO SELFISHNESS, JEALOUSY, PERSONAL HARM IN ALL THREE DIMENSIONS (BODY, MIND, SPIRIT), RELATIONAL DAMAGE, AND EVEN IDOLATRY. HANDLE WITH CARE!

TALK ABOUT IT

1. Where have you seen and experienced one or more of the negative impacts of competition listed in the "warning label"?

2. When you compete "with" someone what would that look like, sound like, and feel like?

3. When you compete "against" someone, what does that look like, sound like, or and feel like?

God's grace is essential if we want to reimagine sports and begin coaching in this newfound way. God's grace is His activity in your life to accomplish what you cannot accomplish on your own.

You will absolutely need God's grace and power in your life to reimagine and move along the transformative journey of rethinking and reforming in the pressurized world of sport. The good news is that He offers His grace freely to us—His sacrifice has already been made on the cross. All we need to do is accept His gift to embark on this journey of faith.

As a group, read the following verses out loud:

> "For you are saved by grace through faith, and this is not from yourselves; it is God's gift—not from works, so that no one can boast."
> —Ephesians 2:8-9

> "But grow in the grace and knowledge of our Lord and Savior Jesus Christ. To him be the glory both now and to the day of eternity."—2 Peter 3:18

> "Rather, train yourself in godliness."
> —1 Timothy 4:7

Although grace is the free gift God gives us as His followers, God wants us to fully participate and cooperate with this transformative process. It is our job to faithfully train ourselves on how to grow in grace. This type of training entails the instituting of practices that put us in a position to receive God's grace.

As we grow in grace, we should be seeing more and more of the activity of God in our lives. As was pointed out in the last video in this lesson, we are three-dimensional beings. Thus, to be the best we can be, we need God's grace and our cooperation with helpful strategies and disciplines to grow in all three dimensions.

TALK ABOUT IT

1. What's the difference between "working out" and "training"?

2. In sports, what role does training play in physical and mental growth?

3. Comparing that to spiritual training and spiritual growth, what are you doing personally to train yourself to be like Jesus?

There is only one true King, and His name is Jesus. Though we are all called to submit to Him first and foremost, Jesus doesn't want us to simply exist as subjects in His Kingdom who are waiting to go to Heaven when we die. We now have the role of ambassadors on his behalf (2 Corinthians 5:20).

When we learn to be ambassadors of His Kingdom in our athletic programs, we can become Kingdom coaches—coaches who seek to live according to the original design for humanity, accurately reflecting God's image and care for His creation on His behalf.

360 COACHING POINT

Live in such a way that those who know you but don't know God will come to know God because they know you.

POST-GAME

MEMORY CHALLENGE

Memorize the following verse for the next meeting:
> "My grace is sufficient for you, for my power is made perfect in weakness."
> —2 Corinthians 12:9

CLOSING PRAYER

Although grace is the free gift God gives us as His followers, God wants us to fully participate and cooperate with this transformative process. It is our job to faithfully train ourselves on how to grow in grace.

Father, as we get started on this journey help us have eyes to see the beauty of life in Your Kingdom. We now open our minds to rethink everything in light of Your good news. We desire to be formed in the likeness of Jesus our King so that whatever needs to change we'll be willing to change. Whatever needs to be abolished will be done away with. Help us center our lives on what is true, what is good, and what is beautiful as we submit our coaching to You.

Purpose

PRE-GAME

Log in to your 360 Coach account and watch the videos for this lesson.

GAME TIME

The world of sports is filled with discussions of success and failure. The most notable form is the scoreboard; it is objective, clear, and measurable—things coaches love. However, if you define success in this way, you are at the mercy of two things you don't control: the outcome and the performance of your players! There's a much better way to determine success: the fulfilling of a clearly defined purpose.

As Christians, our measure of purpose goes beyond a win, a position, or a title. It stems from our Head Coach, our Creator. Romans 8:28-29 tells us, "We know that all things work together for the good of those who love God, who are called according to his purpose. For those he foreknew he also predestined to be conformed to the image of his Son, so that he would be the firstborn among many brothers and sisters."

Take some time to discuss this Scripture as a group.

TALK ABOUT IT

1. What do these verses tell us about God's purpose for us?

2. Do you think times of success or adversity help you to fulfill God's will for your life and become like His Son?

3. Is becoming more like Christ a priority for you? How can it become more of a focus?

4. What elements of your coaching lead you to be more Christ-like? What parts tend to move you in the other direction?

19th century missionary and social reformer William Carey once said, "I'm not afraid of failure; I'm afraid of succeeding at things that don't matter."

When we focus on success as defined by the people and ideology of this world, our view of real, true purpose is clouded.

Take a few minutes and discuss this concept of "purpose" as a group.

TALK ABOUT IT

1. In what ways does sport offer you opportunities to succeed in things that don't matter?

2. What measure of success have you used as a coach?

3. How does fulfilling your purpose factor into that definition?

Most people live their lives focused on WHAT they do and HOW they do it without ever really getting to their WHY. Similarly, most coaches start with WHAT, rush to the HOW, and never bother with the WHY. But how can we know what each is? Let's break this down:

WHAT: Your job description, the task at hand, or your To-Do list
HOW: Your strategy
WHY: Your vision that expresses your purpose

You're not a generic member of God's family, interchangeable with anyone else. God is shaping and preparing you to play a unique role in His world.

God wants your coaching to have a purpose that will bring Him glory, share His grace, and extend His reign. We need to use Scripture to help craft and articulate our purpose by creating a concise statement that explains why God made us.

Your purpose gives meaning and anchors you. As Christians, we believe our identity and purpose should always be built upon the solid foundation of what the Bible says about who God intends His followers to be.

Your purpose declares why God made you. It defines your life, but it focuses on what God thinks.

It anchors your life in the character and call of God. It identifies what never changes about who you are, regardless of circumstances.

As a group, read the following verses out loud:
"Everyone who bears my name and is created for my glory. I have formed them; indeed, I have made them." —Isaiah 43:7

"For we are his workmanship, created in Christ Jesus for good works, which God prepared ahead of time for us to do." —Ephesians 2:10

As a group, take a few minutes to discuss the verses with the questions below.

TALK ABOUT IT

1. What does Isaiah 43:7 say about your purpose?

2. Are you walking in that purpose?

3. Why, according to Ephesians 2:10, were you created?

4. In what ways are you fulfilling that?

5. In light of these verses, WHY do you coach?

6. What would you like your coaching legacy to be?

When we limit our focus to the purpose God designed for us, we can clearly see the WHY of our lives. Establishing this WHY as coaches, who lead our teams in victory and defeat, will equip and empower us to be better role models for our athletes and peers.

POST-GAME

MEMORY CHALLENGE
Before our next meeting, memorize Ephesians 2:10.

CLOSING PRAYER
As we close in prayer today, think about how you can ready yourself to receive God's instruction.

Lord Jesus, I want to fulfill the purpose for which You created me. May that desire override the desire for any success that is not eternal. May my life and coaching bring You glory. In Jesus' name. Amen.

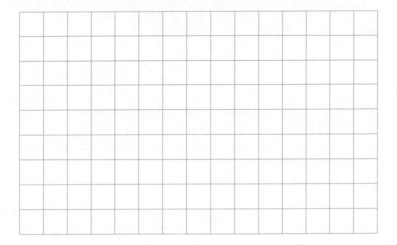

Identity

PRE-GAME

Log in to your 360 Coach account and watch the videos for this lesson.

GAME TIME

One of the driving questions of human existence is, "Who am I?" This question is one of identity, and the answer becomes the cornerstone upon which all else is built. As was pointed out at the beginning of the first video in this lesson, there are multiple levels to that question.

If you were to answer, "I am a mom, dad, wife, husband, brother, plumber, teacher, coach..." those would certainly be legitimate answers; however, all those aspects of our identities cannot become the core of who we are.

When we align ourselves with God and what God has to say, it's a little easier to answer the question of who we are becoming. In 2 Corinthians 5:17-21, we read about where our identity stems from:

> Therefore, if anyone is in Christ, he is a new creation; the old has passed away, and see, the new has come! Everything is from God, who has reconciled us to himself through Christ and has given us the ministry of reconciliation. That is, in Christ, God was reconciling the world to himself, not counting their trespasses against them, and he has committed the message of reconciliation to us.

> Therefore, we are ambassadors for Christ, since God is making his appeal through us. We plead on Christ's behalf, 'Be reconciled to God.' He made the one who did not know sin to be sin for us, so that in him we might become the righteousness of God.

Take a few minutes to reread the passage above. Then, as a group, take five minutes and discuss the questions below.

TALK ABOUT IT

1. Paul says that in Christ, we have moved from old ways into new ways. What is our new identity in Christ?

2. How does this new identity affect all other areas of our lives, especially coaching?

Remember Coach Jane from the video? As she recounted, the more deeply invested she became in her performance as a coach, the more coaching encroached upon her core identity. The challenge for Christ-followers is to be on guard against allowing what we do to replace who and whose we are.

God's original design was for our doing to flow from our being. The subtle lie of the enemy and the temptation of our sinful natures is to reverse that design. As Coach Jane noted, everything came into alignment when her role as a coach became rightly related to her identity as a child of God.

TALK ABOUT IT

1. Are you tempted to find your identity in your performance or the performance of your athletes? If so, in what ways?

a. Read 1 John 5:1-5.

2. In Christ, we become children of God. What does John say we do in response to who we are?

a. Read Galatians 3:25-28.

3. What happens to all our other identities when we come to Christ? What does this mean for you as a coach?

This journey of becoming a Kingdom coach is a life-long pursuit of coming back repeatedly to the reality of our core identity as a son or daughter of the King of Kings—Jesus Christ. We must push back against the temptation to find our significance or self-worth in anything or anyone else. Out of our rightly related identity in Christ comes a beautiful path of joyfully working and serving Him and His Kingdom.

Take a few minutes to read Ephesians 2:1-10 as a group. Then, go back and reread the passage to yourself, underlining or highlighting what stands out to you. Discuss the questions below as a group.

> And you were dead in your trespasses
> and sins in which you previously walked

according to the ways of this world, according to the ruler of the power of the air, the spirit now working in the disobedient. We too all previously lived among them in our fleshly desires, carrying out the inclinations of our flesh and thoughts, and we were by nature children under wrath as the others were also. But God, who is rich in mercy, because of his great love that he had for us, made us alive with Christ even though we were dead in trespasses. You are saved by grace!
He also raised us up with him and seated us with him in the heavens in Christ Jesus, so that in the coming ages he might display the immeasurable riches of his grace through his kindness to us in Christ Jesus. For you are saved by grace through faith, and this is not from yourselves; it is God's gift—not from works, so that no one can boast. For we are his workmanship, created in Christ Jesus for good works, which God prepared ahead of time for us to do.

TALK ABOUT IT

1. What was our identity before we were in Christ?

2. Notice the "But God" transition in verse 4. What is true now that God has saved us in Christ?

3. What is Paul saying about what God has done for us? For what purpose have we been given this new identity?

4. What would it look like for you to view your coaching as an arena in which to do the good works God has prepared for you?

When we focus on whose we are from God, we discern exactly who we are and what our purpose is.

360 COACHING POINT

Your core identity is a redeemed child of God whom He loves. You must be continually on guard against allowing performance to become your core identity.

POST-GAME

MEMORY CHALLENGE
Before our next meeting, memorize the following verse:

> "I am the gate. If anyone enters by me,
> he will be saved and will come in and go
> out and find pasture. A thief comes only
> to steal and kill and destroy. I have come
> so that they may have life and have it in
> abundance." —John 10:9-10

CLOSING PRAYER
As we close in prayer today, think about how you can ready yourself to receive God's instruction.

Lord, help me always remember who I am based upon whose I am: I am a child of the King! In Christ, You have made me a new creation. May all I do flow out of this reality. As I relate to others, may I reflect on this truth. Help me to live securely in this since nothing can separate me from Your love. Amen.

EXTRA CREDIT
Take multiple brightly colored Post-it notes and write "I am a child of God for whom He loves." Stick them around your house, in your car, in your office, and in the locker room to remind you of your true identity. By the next meeting, be ready to discuss how you felt when you read this truth as you went through your day.

Values

PRE-GAME

Log in to your 360 Coach account and watch the videos for this lesson.

GAME TIME

Values are essential to effective leadership. Here's a simple definition: "Values are norms or principles which guide our interactions and convictions." They are motivational, giving us the reason why we do things; and they are restrictive, acting as guardrails for decisions and behaviors.

Values are those things we deem important that provide direction and guidance despite our emotions. As you coach, you are striving to build these norms or principles in your athletes.

Take a few minutes to talk about the concept of value in your life and in your role as a coach.

TALK ABOUT IT

1. As you examine your own life and career, what values do you see as driving your behavior?

2. List three top values you are striving to build in your athletes. Give a quick explanation as to why these are your top three.

3. What value do you best live out in front of your athletes? In what ways is that demonstrated?

Showing values to your athletes as you coach depends a lot on your awareness and ability to live out core values in your daily life. Sports involvement, and your impact as a coach, **will impart** a set of values to your athletes. But this requires constant, deliberate *reflection* and *implementation*.

When we pray "in Jesus' name," we are invoking the character and the values that Jesus represented. We are ambassadors of Christ. As ambassadors, we learn to think like He would think and act as He would act because we value what He values. When we are under stress, our values become apparent. And since sports can have all sorts of stress points, our values will be made visible.

It would be wise to have your values worked through and agreed upon at the very start before stress points make them visible.

Let's look at two stress points in Jesus' life: one at the beginning of His ministry and one at a crucial point of decision. As a group, take a few minutes to read Matthew 4:1-11 and Mark 14:32-36. Then, discuss the questions below together.

TALK ABOUT IT

1. Go back to Matthew 4:1-11 Mark 14:32-36. What values does Jesus represent?

2. How can we implement these values in our worldof sports?

Research shows that the general sports experience tends to build performance character but also erodes moral character. This is because the sports world honors winners. It values winning. It values results over process.

This is a great danger in all things competitive—sports, business, and even politics. When we greatly desire the outcome of something and aren't focused on who we are or what we do to get there, we can easily forget the process and only focus on the outcome. Thankfully, we have a great example in Jesus that we can follow. When we focus on Jesus and His teachings, we have an example to follow that reminds us that the process is the outcome in the making.

In Mark 8:36-37, Jesus says, "For what does it benefit someone to gain the whole world and yet lose his life? What can anyone give in exchange for his life?"

When the result we are striving for is used as justification for means we know God would not endorse, we are in danger of forfeiting our soul.

With this in mind, let's discuss the process that Coach Wilmeth went through as she and her team established a set of core values. Rewatch Coach Wilmeth's video (4b), and as you watch, think about your answers to the questions below.

TALK ABOUT IT

1. As you listened to Coach Wilmeth share the process of choosing core values with her team, what stood out to you? Explain your reasoning.

2. As you listened to the assistant coach who wrestled with the core value of integrity when he played, what stood out to you? Explain your reasoning.

3. What situations do you find yourself in where your competitive spirit could conflict with your core values? What about when those values are in conflict with the Holy Spirit?

4. Where could this "honor call" example from the video apply in your sport and your coaching?

When you deliberately align your core values with that of Jesus and His teachings, the example that you are setting as a coach goes far beyond the scoreboard. As you compete today, remember that Jesus is the ultimate example to follow. When we mirror Him, we're doing Kingdom work.

> ### 360 COACHING POINT
> *Values serve to guard your heart and keep you focused on the process rather than the result.*

POST-GAME

1. List your core four values.
2. At your next practice or event, ask your players to list the things they think you value as it relates to your team and sport. See if what they say lines up with what you wrote or want.

MEMORY CHALLENGE
Before our next meeting, memorize the following verse:

> I have been crucified with Christ and I no longer live, but Christ lives in me. The life I now live in the body, I live by faith in the Son of God, who loved me and gave himself for me. —Galatians 2:20

CLOSING PRAYER

As we close in prayer today, think about how you can ready yourself to receive God's instruction.

Lord, thank You for my role as Your ambassador. Help me to get clarity on what that looks like in sport. Help me to value the things most valuable in Your Kingdom. Guide me as I focus on the process of what I am becoming and what I am helping my players become. Let me keep winning in its proper place. Train me to keep my competitive spirit submitted to Your Holy Spirit. May my legacy, what I leave behind with my players, be one based on truth, goodness, and beauty. Amen.

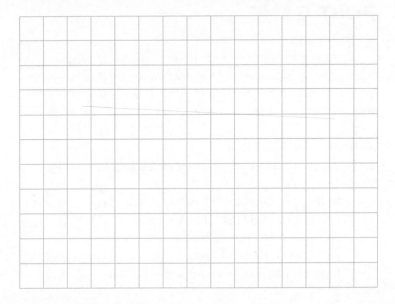

Character

PRE-GAME

Log in to your 360 Coach account and watch the videos for this lesson.

GAME TIME

Sport is both character building and character revealing. Character is the essential nature of something or someone. We are called to put on the character of Christ. Being a disciple is not a process of learning what the teacher knows. It's the process of becoming like the teacher. As a group, read 2 Peter 1:3-8 together. Then, discuss the associated questions.

> His divine power has given us everything required for life and godliness through the knowledge of him who called us by his own glory and goodness. By these he has given us very great and precious promises, so that through them you may share in the divine nature, escaping the corruption

that is in the world because of evil desire. For this very reason, make every effort to supplement your faith with goodness, goodness with knowledge, knowledge with self-control, self-control with endurance, endurance with godliness, godliness with brotherly affection, and brotherly affection with love. For if you possess these qualities in increasing measure, they will keep you from being useless or unfruitful in the knowledge of our Lord Jesus Christ.

TALK ABOUT IT

1. What does it mean to "participate in the divine nature"? How does this apply to our lives as coaches?

2. If God has given us "everything we need for a godly life," why are we then told to "make every effort" toward building the eight character attributes listed?

3. What would it look like to "make every effort" with these eight attributes in your coaching?

In video 5a, we address the two categories of character: Performance Character and Moral Character.

Performance Character acts like fuel to get us to our goal. It is what makes for a great performance.

Moral Character acts like a compass, keeping us headed in the right direction. It is what makes us good.

It can be said that "greatness" is the evaluation of the quality of our work (what we do), and "goodness" is the evaluation of the essence of it (who we are). A big issue in sports is that we are more enamored by greatness than we are by goodness.

In Genesis 1:31, we read, "God saw all that he had made, and it was very good indeed." As great as the original creation was, it's telling that God, as the master artist of creation, called His original creation "good." The focal point of the original creation was when God, the Father, created mankind in His own image through Jesus Christ. Our ability to be creative is one of the primary ways we possess a likeness to God.

Take a few minutes to discuss the questions below as a group.

TALK ABOUT IT

1. What are some of the similarities between a coach and an artist?

2. In what ways does the program you are creating resemble a work of art?

As the creators of our sports programs who are molding the lives of athletes, it's important to understand the categorical differences between good and great. Not only is it important that we understand the difference, but we also need to understand where "goodness" comes from.

Take a few minutes to read Luke 6:43-45 as a group. Then, reread the passage individually, thinking about the essence of goodness.

"A good tree doesn't produce bad fruit; on the other hand, a bad tree doesn't produce good fruit. For each tree is known by its own fruit. Figs aren't gathered from thornbushes, or grapes picked from a bramble bush. A good person produces good out of the good stored up in his heart. An evil person produces evil out of the evil stored up in his heart, for his mouth speaks from the overflow of the heart. A good man produces good out of the good storeroom of his heart. An evil man produces evil out of the evil storeroom, for his mouth speaks from the overflow of the heart."

TALK ABOUT IT

1. According to this passage, where does "good" and "evil" come from?

2. How can this teaching of Christ instruct our efforts in coaching?

If we want to unlock the hidden treasures of the good and the great to produce beauty in sports, we must learn to harness the power of love in our programs.

The most powerful, motivating force in the universe is love. As coaches who seek to tap into this motivating power, it is important to have an accurate definition of the type of love that is being referred to.

The Apostle Paul gave a clear and compelling description of love in his letter to the church at Corinth:

> Love is patient, love is kind. Love does not envy, is not boastful, is not arrogant, is not rude, is not self-seeking, is not irritable, and does not keep a record of wrongs. Love finds no joy in unrighteousness but rejoices in the truth. It bears all things, believes all things, hopes all things, endures all things. —1 Corinthians 13:4-7

Take a few minutes to discuss the questions below as they relate to the passage.

TALK ABOUT IT

1. How many character attributes are listed in definition of love in the verse above? Which of them would be "performance" attributes and which would be "moral"?

2. In the description of love in 1 Corinthians 13:4-7, which of the character attributes listed jump out as those that can help a person pursue and persist in sports and in life? Discuss.

360 COACHING POINT

"Do your little bit of good where you are; it's those little bits of good put together that over-whelm the world." —Desmond Tutu

POST-GAME

MEMORY VERSE

Before the next meeting, memorize the following verse:

> "A good person produces good out of the good stored up in his heart." —Luke 6:45

CLOSING PRAYER

As we close in prayer today, think about how you can ready yourself to receive God's instruction.

Father God, thank You for Your good creation and thank You for our opportunity to be co-creators with You. Help us to be intentional about coaching the goodness of God along with the greatness of sport, so that we can produce pockets of beauty that are a foreshadow of Your beautiful Kingdom that is coming with the return of Your Son, Jesus. We ask this in the name of Jesus our Messiah. Amen!

Motivation

PRE-GAME

Log in to your 360 Coach account and watch the videos for this lesson.

GAME TIME

Motivation can be described as the inclination to pursue and persist in the journey toward a desired outcome. As coaches, we all want motivated athletes because getting better at our sport and learning new things is hard work! It's uncomfortable. The sacrifices necessary can be very costly in time, effort, money, or relationships. "Is it worth the price?" "What am I doing this for?" "Why am I doing this?" At its core, this is a motivational issue.

TALK ABOUT IT

1. As a group, list all the things used to motivate athletes (be specific).

2. Are some good? Are some bad? Why or why not?

There are a lot of different things that motivate people: pride, jealousy, fear, anger, and so on. Though these motivators can get short-term results, they inevitably can harm us or others. But here's the good news. There's a motivator that does no harm and is considered the most powerful motivating force in the universe. **This is love.**

Love is not a feeling, it is a divine way of relating to others, and ourselves, that moves through every dimension of our being and orients the world toward what is good, true, and beautiful.

Love is not about intensity. It is about consistency. We learn about the most important aspects of love through Jesus Christ and His Word.

As a group, read Galatians 6:9-10 together. Then, answer the questions below.

> Let us not get tired of doing good, for we will reap at the proper time if we don't give up. Therefore, as we have opportunity, let us work for the good of all, especially for those who belong to the household of faith.

TALK ABOUT IT

1. What causes you to get weary or lose motivation during your season?

2. What indications do you look for when your team or players are losing their motivation to pursue and persist?

A simple principle that coaches can enact to help intrinsically motivate players is simply this: step into the athlete's life away from the athletic environment. Do things that show them you care about them as a person and not just as a player.

Take a few minutes to brainstorm some ideas about what this might look like for your team.

As we think about what may motivate our athletes, let's look at an example from Jesus. As a group, read the passage from Luke 19:1-10 below. Then, take a few minutes to discuss the associated questions.

He entered Jericho and was passing through. There was a man named Zacchaeus who was a chief tax collector, and he was rich. He was trying to see who Jesus was, but he was not able because of the crowd, since he was a short man. So running ahead, he climbed up a sycamore tree to see Jesus, since he was about to pass that way. When Jesus came to the place, he looked up and said to him, 'Zacchaeus, hurry and come down because today it is necessary for me to stay at your house.'

So he quickly came down and welcomed him joyfully. All who saw it began to complain, 'He's gone to stay with a sinful man.'

But Zacchaeus stood there and said to the Lord, 'Look, I'll give half of my possessions to the poor, Lord. And if I have extorted anything from anyone, I'll pay back four times as much.'

'Today salvation has come to this house,' Jesus told him, 'because he too is a son of Abraham. For the Son of Man has come to seek and to save the lost.'

TALK ABOUT IT

1. How does the motivation of love fit into Jesus' visit to the home of Zaccheaus?

2. When Jesus went to Zacchaeus' house, what impact did it have on him?

Zacchaeus was known as a traitor by his countrymen because he extorted taxes from his own people and gave them to the Roman government while keeping plenty of the money for himself.

Jesus had an interest in changing Zacchaeus' motives and behavior, but He didn't try to change them by extrinsically issuing threats or warnings of punishment. Instead, Jesus desired to change Zacchaeus' heart by establishing a relationship with him that was solely based on **the love of God**.

What Jesus did for Zacchaeus, He did for all of us when joined us in humanity and took on our sins.

Take a few minutes to read the passages below individually. Then, come back together as a group and discuss the associated questions.

> "The Word became flesh and dwelt among us. We observed his glory, the glory as the one and only Son from the Father, full of grace and truth." —John 1:14

> "For God loved the world in this way: He gave his one and only Son, so that everyone who believes in him will not perish but have eternal life. For God did not send his Son into the world to condemn the world, but to save the world through him." —John 3:16-17

> "See! I stand at the door and knock. If anyone hears my voice and opens the door, I will come in to him and eat with him, and he with me." —Revelation 3:20

TALK ABOUT IT

1. According to these two passages, why did Jesus come into the world?

2. What does John 3:16-17 reveal about God's disposition towards humanity?

3. Does this understanding help motivate you to follow Jesus? Is the motivation more intrinsic or extrinsic? Why?

4. When looking back at the passage in Revelations, what does it mean to hear His voice and let Him in?

When we motivate others and our players with love rather than fear of punishment or infatuation with bribery, their performance and their drive for excellence on and off their field, court, or arena of play, becomes more solidified and longer lasting.

POST-GAME

MEMORY VERSE

Before our next meeting, memorize the following verse:

> "For God loved the world in this way: He gave his one and only Son, so that everyone who believes in him will not perish but have eternal life." —John 3:16

CLOSING PRAYER

As we close in prayer today, think about how you can ready yourself to receive God's instruction.

Lord Jesus, because of Your vast love for us, You came and visited us in our mortality, that we might attain eternal life through faith in You. Thank You for pursuing us in the incarnation and persisting to bring us back into a right relationship with You through the work of the cross. Help us model this simple action with our players in an effort to build relationships with them. May this simple act help them become intrinsically motivated to pursue excellence in our sport and a deeper relationship with You and others. Amen.

Confidence

PRE-GAME

Log in to your 360 Coach account and watch the videos for this lesson.

GAME TIME

Confidence may be the most influential psychological contributor to success on the playing field for an athlete or a team. Confidence can be defined as an individual's belief that he or she has the necessary skills to produce a desired outcome.

Thus, confidence exists in the present by looking back in belief (faith) and looking forward to the desired outcome (hope).

As a group, take a few minutes to discuss the questions below.

TALK ABOUT IT

1. Share a story about a time when confidence, or the lack of confidence, drastically impacted the athletic performance of either yourself or of an athlete you have coached.

2. What were some of the contributing factors?

The writer of Hebrews gives some great advice on how we can gain or regain confidence: by holding on to **hope** (future), remembering the **faithfulness** of God (past actions), connecting with others in the community, and promoting **love** (motivation) and good works to one another.

Let's look at a specific example in text.

As a group, read the following verse together. Then, take a few minutes to read it to yourself individually, highlighting or underlining things that stick out to you.

> Let us hold on to the confession of our hope without wavering, since he who

promised is faithful. And let us consider
one another in order to provoke love and
good works, not neglecting to gather
together, as some are in the habit of doing,
but encouraging each other, and all the
more as you see the day approaching.
—Hebrews 10:23-25

The ingredients of true confidence are faith, hope, and love. Faith exists in the present by first looking backward.

Faith is reason-based and evidence-based. The more reasons you can give, the more established your belief, thus the more robust your confidence.

Faith works in three directions: inward, outward, and upward.
- Inward: **You**.
  What reasons or evidence do you have that you're prepared for the contest?
- Outward: **Others**.
  What reasons or evidence do you have that your players and coaches can be trusted and are prepared?
- Upward: **God**.
  What reasons or what evidence would you give for your faith in Jesus? Why submit your life to Him?

When we establish our faith, we can focus on hope. Hope is more than just a state of mind; it is an action-oriented strength. Hope is a present expectation of future good. Hope's function is to keep the present reality open to a future possibility. Hope exists in the present. It looks forward to a future good.

The thing that separates the basic definition of hope and the biblical definition of hope is what we'll call The God Factor. Your hope should be based on the fact of who God is and what He promises for those who have put their faith in Him. After all, that is what His promises are designed to do—inspire hope.

Let's look at another verse that joins the principles of hope and faith together.

> "Now faith is the reality of what is hoped
> for, the proof of what is not seen."
> —Hebrews 11:1

This verse ties together hope and faith. In essence, you have hope because you have faith and you have faith because you have hope.

Your entire walk as a believer is based on hope: hope that goes beyond this life and extends throughout eternity. Everything you do as a Christian flows from this. Why do you pray? Hope. Why do you witness? Hope. Why do you endure hardship, trials, or persecution? Hope. Why did many who have gone before us sacrifice, give, serve, even lose their lives for the message of the Gospel? One word—hope.

TALK ABOUT IT

1. In your opinion, what does a hopeful person look and sound like?

2. What promises of Jesus give you the greatest hope and power in the present?

3. What future hopes do you have (for your sport, your life, this world) that give you power in the present?

What holds faith and hope together in the present? It's love. It's the magnetic force that holds the past and future together. Love gives meaning to present activities and relationships. It motivates us to act on our beliefs as we move in future hope.

While it is your job to build confidence in your players, it's important to distinguish between confidence and arrogance. There is a fine line between the two, and most often the difference is the character attribute of humility.

Let's take a look at Scripture that directly addresses the issue of the importance of humility. Then, as a group, discuss the associated questions.

> In the same way, you who are younger, be subject to the elders. All of you clothe yourselves with humility toward one another, because God resists the proud but gives grace to the humble.
>
> Humble yourselves, therefore, under the mighty hand of God, so that he may exalt you at the proper time, casting all your cares on him, because he cares about you.
> —1 Peter 5:5-7

TALK ABOUT IT

1. What is the relationship between humility and confidence in this passage?

2. What does God promise to the humble? What will He do to the proud?

POST-GAME

MEMORY VERSE

Before our next meeting, memorize the following verse:

> "I am sure of this, that he who started a good work in you will carry it on to completion until the day of Christ Jesus."
> — Philippians 1:6

CLOSING PRAYER

As we close in prayer today, think about how you can ready yourself to receive God's instruction.

King Jesus, direct our focus first and foremost on who You are, what You've done for us, and what You promise for those who are called according to Your purpose. May faith, hope, and love direct our interactions with You and with our players. By Your Spirit, help us to remember the brokenness that many of our athletes are feeling inside due to the pressures and situations they are facing in the culture. Grant that we might help them to maintain or regain a sense of confidence by the way we demonstrate Your love to them, regardless of how well they perform. Amen.

Emotions

PRE-GAME

Log in to your 360 Coach account and watch the videos for this lesson.

GAME TIME

The whole range of human emotions is regularly put on display through competition in sports. The thrill of victory, the agony of defeat, and everything in between, is regularly felt on fields of play all around the world.

TALK ABOUT IT

1. What is the most passionate display of emotions you have ever felt or witnessed as either a coach or a player?

2. Think about this statement for a minute: **Emotions are powerful servants, but they are lousy masters.** How can you relate to this?

It should be the goal of every coach to help athletes gain mastery over their emotions so that they can help rather than harm their athletic performance.

This begins with a coach's personal awareness of their own emotional responses and the effect those have on their coaching and their athletes.

If you explode every time a referee makes a bad call, are you setting a good example for your players? Not at all. You're showing your players how to treat others with disrespect, which is in direct conflict with God's second part of the most important commandment (according to Jesus):

> "The second is like it: Love your neighbor as yourself." —Matthew 22:39

When you align yourself with the likeness of Christ and gain mastery in this area, you can help your athletes become aware, take control, and practice responding accordingly.

This cannot be done by direct effort because emotions are not primary, they are secondary. Emotions are a response. They are a response to our thoughts, consciousness, or otherwise.

For our purposes as coaches, we need to understand that emotions are a response to our thinking about our performance. This is one reason why Scripture puts so much focus on our thought life.

As a group, read the following verses out loud:

> "We demolish arguments and every proud thing that is raised up against the knowledge of God, and we take every thought captive to obey Christ."
> —2 Corinthians 10:5

> "Finally brothers and sisters, whatever is true, whatever is honorable, whatever is just, whatever is pure, whatever is lovely, whatever is commendable—if there is any moral excellence and if there is anything praiseworthy—dwell on these things."
> —Philippians 4:8

> "Set your minds on things above, not on earthly things." —Colossians 3:2

TALK ABOUT IT

1. Take thoughts captive, think on these things, and set your mind on the things above. What would coaching look like, feel like, and sound like when this is your focus?

2. What strategies or disciplines can you think of that will help you do this?

Have someone read 1 Corinthians 10:23-24 to the group out loud. Individually, take five minutes to work through the passage. Then, come back as a group and discuss what you found interesting.

> "'Everything is permissible,' but not everything is beneficial. 'Everything is permissible,' but not everything builds up. No one is to seek his own good, but the good of the other person."
> —1 Corinthians 10:23-24

In this passage, Paul deals with what is permissible for a Christian. At the time, he was specifically addressing the question about whether or not it was okay for Christians to eat food that had been previously sacrificed to idols. People had differing opinions on this issue.

Rather than fanning the flames of controversy, Paul reframed the issue not on the basis of clear-cut right and wrong, but around the idea that even if something is permissible it should be governed by the greater **law of love**.

As this translates into coaching, it is important to realize that although short-term anger or frustration may "work" at motivating your players, these tactics should always be governed by love.

As a coach who is desiring to get the most out of your players, frustration will certainly be an emotion you will experience from time to time. Frustration can quickly become disappointment or anger depending upon the relationship you have with your players.

When the coach-player relationships are strong on a team, showing disappointment might be a better display of emotions than even short-term anger.

TALK ABOUT IT

1. What is the difference between anger and disappointment?

2. Read Proverbs 29:11 and James 1:19-20. What do these verses show us about controlling our emotions?

3. Which of these passages motivates you to improve more?

It is not easy to retrain our thoughts or to respond in Christ-like ways. Through the Holy Spirit who lives in us, we are empowered to focus our minds on the right things. It will become easier.

You can develop a new frame of reference based on what is true, noble, right, pure, lovely, admirable, excellent, and praiseworthy.

As you continue coaching this week, we challenge you to execute the following plays for yourself:

1. *Reflect*. Sit with Jesus. Ask the Holy Spirit to help you reflect on your emotional responses and discern the thoughts behind them.
2. *Practice gratitude*. Gratitude and fear cannot coexist, so focus on the former when coaching this week.
3. *Create an environment that is marked by joy*. Effort and perseverance flow from joy.

> ## 360 COACHING POINT
> *"The ultimate freedom we have as human beings is the power to select what we will allow or require our minds to dwell on."* —Dallas Willard

POST-GAME

MEMORY CHALLENGE
Memorize the following verse for the next meeting:
"I have told you these things so that my joy may be in you and your joy may be complete." —John 15:11

CLOSING PRAYER

As we close in prayer today, think about how you can ready yourself to receive God's instruction.

Father God, You know all of our deepest areas of struggle when it comes to channeling our emotions in a way that not only helps performance but also helps our athletes become the type of men and women You want them to become. Help us, by the power of Your Spirit, to demonstrate all of Your characteristics as we seek to coach the way You have called us to coach. Thank You for the opportunity to influence the lives of so many. Help us to use our influence in a way that helps us and our players become more like You and brings glory to Your name. We ask these things in the name of Your Son, Jesus. Amen!

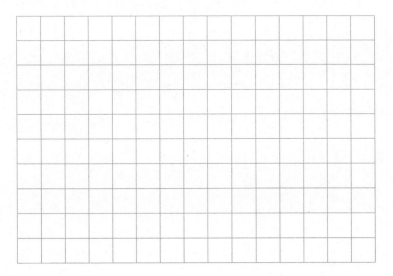

Team Cohesion

PRE-GAME

Log in to your 360 Coach account and watch the videos for this lesson.

GAME TIME

How you take a bunch of "me" and make them into a "we" is the task of every coach who wants a cohesive team. Jesus' situation was no different. Jesus had parent issues that threatened team cohesion (Matthew 20:20-21). He had members of his team jockeying for the best positions and privileges. Let's look at one of those:

> They came to Capernaum. When he was in the house, he asked them, 'What were you arguing about on the way?' But they were silent, because on the way they had been arguing with one another about who was the greatest. —Mark 9:33-34

This account of the disciples of Christ could describe the interaction (or at least the thoughts) of many teams. Who is the real MVP of this team? Sport offers as many opportunities for conflict as it does unity. Words like competition, matchup, rivalry, antagonism, contest, conflict, fight, jealousy, envy, etc. can just as easily define the relationships within a team as it does the interaction with the opponent.

Take a few minutes to read through the passage again and discuss the following questions:

TALK ABOUT IT

1. Would you describe the discussion of the disciples on who was the greatest as audacious? Why or why not?

2. Describe how you think the disciples' argument affected their relationships.

3. Rather than seeking greatness, what is a better focus for the Christ-follower?

The current of the river of sport flows very strongly downstream toward individual goals, success, and accolades. To build team cohesion, one must intentionally go against the current and paddle upstream.

TALK ABOUT IT

1. How does striving for individual success challenge building team cohesion?

2. How can a parent's expectations for their child as an individual player test team unity?

3. Do you have any personal goals or aspirations as a coach that might prevent you from enjoying life-giving relationships with your athletes, their parents, or opposing coaches?

The culture of sport is often one of comparing and competing. But as Theodore Roosevelt once said, "Comparison is the thief of joy."

In John 10:10, Jesus says, "A thief comes only to steal and kill and destroy. I have come so that they may have life and have it in abundance."

Joy and life are stolen, killed, and destroyed from sport with an unhealthy understanding of competition. We learned in the first lesson that there are two different approaches to competition. We either compete with each other or against each other. Each path we take affects team cohesion.

TALK ABOUT IT

1. When competition is viewed as against one another and becomes an exercise in self-interest, describe how the following are affected:

a. Goal setting

b. Motivation

c. Emotions

d. Confidence

e. Team cohesion

2. Coach, what is the thief trying to steal, kill, and destroy in your coaching?

3. Would you describe your sports experience as the "rich and satisfying life" that Jesus stated He wants for you?

4. What about the experience of your players?

It is clear throughout Scripture that God wants us to demonstrate love for one another and experience unity. In fact, Jesus states in John 13:35 that this demonstrated love for one another "...everyone will know that you are my disciples..."

These life-giving relationships based on love are pleasing to God and we too get to enjoy their fruit.

The resulting team cohesion is a beautiful taste of that "rich and satisfying life."

POST-GAME

MEMORY CHALLENGE
Memorize the following verse for the next meeting:
> "I give you a new command: Love one another. Just as I have loved you, you are also to love one another. By this everyone will know that you are my disciples, if you love one another."—John 13:34-35

CLOSING PRAYER
As we close in prayer today, think about how you can ready yourself to receive God's instruction.

Lord, I thank You that we have been designed to be part of a team, the body of Christ. We cannot succeed on our own. May our competitive spirit submit to Your Holy Spirit so that we will strive together and serve one another in love. Let gratitude

*and humility be the hallmarks of our coaching. In
Jesus' name. Amen.*

EXTRA CREDIT
Write the following verses on a 3x5 card and keep it
where you will see it regularly.

> Let each person examine his own work,
> and then he can take pride in himself
> alone, and not compare himself with
> someone else. For each person will have
> to carry his own load. —Galatians 6:4-5

The Physical Body

PRE-GAME

Log in to your 360 Coach account and watch the videos for this lesson.

GAME TIME

Because we are physical beings, spiritual truths are best lived out in bodies that are well cared for.

Let's go back to the jug illustration that was started in the first lesson and ended in the last video. The pressures of the sports world to conform to its standards in stewarding our physical bodies are intense.

Study after study continues to confirm what many parents and coaches have known to be anecdotally true: For too many athletes, the sports journey is damaging to their physical well-being. Overuse injuries and high-impact injuries are steadily on the rise amongst athletes ages 8-18. Risk-reward conversations in light of the high priority and dignity God bestows on the body are rarely, if ever, addressed by followers of Jesus in the sports world.

We started this journey in lesson one with the start of Jesus' ministry: Jesus' announcement. It's only appropriate that we come back to it in this last lesson:

> After John was arrested, Jesus went to Galilee, proclaiming the good news of God: 'The time is fulfilled, and the kingdom of God has come near. Repent and believe the good news!' —Mark 1:14-15

In this announcement, Jesus is telling us we need to repent, rethink everything, and then believe, arranging our lives and actions around this new reality.

When Jesus returns to fully institute His Kingship (His presidency of the world), assuming sport has a place in God's Kingdom and a new government, Romans 12:1-2 can help us rethink what sports should look like with a distinctly Christian imagination. Read this Scripture together, and answer the questions that follow.

> Therefore, brothers and sisters, in view of the mercies of God, I urge you to present your bodies as a living sacrifice, holy and pleasing to God; this is your true worship. Do not be conformed to this age, but be transformed by the renewing of your mind, so that you may discern what is the good, pleasing, and perfect will of God.
> —Romans 12:1-2

TALK ABOUT IT

If we desire to coach under the rule and reign of King Jesus, renewing our minds around God's good design for our physical bodies and their intended limits is imperative.

As a group, read the following Scriptures together:

"Then the LORD God formed the man out of the dust from the ground and breathed the breath of life into his nostrils, and the man became a living being." —Genesis 2:7

"Then God said, 'Let us make man in our image, according to our likeness. They will rule the fish of the sea, the birds of the sky, the livestock, the whole earth, and the creatures that crawl on the earth.' So God created man in his own image; he created him in the image of God; he created them male and female." —Genesis 2:22-23

"The Word became flesh and dwelt among us. We observed his glory, the glory as the one and only Son from the Father, full of grace and truth." —John 1:14

"But as it is, Christ has been raised from the dead, the firstfruits of those who have fallen asleep. For since death came through a man, the resurrection of the dead also comes through a man. For just as in Adam all die, so also in Christ all will be made alive." —1 Corinthians 15:20-22

In the Genesis account, we see that God created human bodies, and He deemed them very good. When John says, "the Word became flesh," He is describing what theologians call the incarnation.

Jesus, the eternal second person of the Trinitarian God-head, was born into the world with a physical human body. The reality of the incarnation demonstrates the inherent goodness and dignity of human bodies.

In 1 Corinthians 15, Paul tells us that in the same way God raised Jesus from the dead, He will also raise our bodies from the dead at the end of the age. We will spend our eternal lives in the New Creation in new, glorified, and upgraded physical bodies.

TALK ABOUT IT

1. How can these truths impact how we treat our physical bodies?

2. Which Scripture passage stood out to you the most? Why?

"Water makes you weak!"

Most folks chuckle at Coach Boone's hydration philosophy from the movie *Remember the Titans*; however, underestimating, or worse, deliberately violating proper care for our physical bodies is a serious matter. We live in an age where electric lighting, smartphones, cars, planes, and supplements constantly tempt us to blow right past our physical limits, and that temptation only ramps up when we step onto our field of play.

In 1 Corinthians 6:19-20, Paul makes the argument that we should treat our bodies as holy because, well, they are!

TALK ABOUT IT

1. What's the significance of Paul's statements that "you are not your own?"

2. List three ways you can help shape the culture of your program to care well for your players' bodies.

The pressures from the outside can be massive, and the effect is not just physical; it's in all three dimensions. Without strategies and resources to push back against that pressure from the inside, it will deform us.

God graciously gives us three things with which to push back and not conform to the pressure:

1. His Word,
2. His Holy Spirit, and
3. His people (the Church).

TALK ABOUT IT

1. Share with each other how each of these, at one time in your coaching journey, has helped you not conform to how the sports world responds.

2. Share one time where you found yourself conformed. What would help you not respond that way in the future?

360 COACHING POINT

God cares deeply about the physical aspect of our being. He desires for coaches and athletes to steward and care for their bodies well.

POST-GAME

MEMORY CHALLENGE

Memorize the following verse for the next meeting:

> Therefore, brothers and sisters, in view of
> the mercies of God, I urge you to present
> your bodies as a living sacrifice, holy and
> pleasing to God; this is your true worship.
> Do not be conformed to this age, but be
> transformed by the renewing of your mind,
> so that you may discern what is the good,
> pleasing, and perfect will of God.
> —Romans 12:1-2

CLOSING PRAYER

As we close in prayer today, think about how you can
ready yourself to receive God's instruction.

*Father, You never meant for us to do this life alone.
You are a God who gives. You've given us Your Word.
You've given us the Holy Spirit and the community
of believers who journey with us. As we end this part
of the journey, may we continue to rethink what we
do in light of Your Word. May we believe, align our
lives (empowered by Your Spirit), and live together in
love so those who see us will know that we are Your
disciples who desire to make more disciples. In Jesus'
name. Amen.*

EXTRA CREDIT

Take a few minutes to write down your opinion on creating a culture of health and care for the physical body. Share it with your Athletic Director, coaching staff, and parents.

TRANSFORMATIONAL PURPOSE STATEMENT

Coach, God is in the process of accomplishing a miraculous work in your life. By grace and faith in Jesus Christ, He is transforming you from the inside out. He redeems you and restores the purpose for which you were created. Now, He gives you a specific calling and sends you on a mission: to see others transformed by Jesus Christ!

The Transformational Purpose Statement is a tool to inspire you every day. It will help keep you focused by maintaining your God-inspired purpose at the center of your coaching. It serves as a constant reminder of the great purpose that God has given you—to center your life and coaching in the Kingdom and to make disciples as you go.

Whether you are writing a first draft or refining an existing statement, take the time necessary to write down words that are thoughtful and well-crafted. As you complete this exercise, consider the following suggestions to help you write an effective Transformational Purpose Statement.

1. **Be Authentic:** This is your personal statement. Don't write what you think you're supposed to say or copy someone else's statement. Rather, write in your own words what reflects your heart. The first draft doesn't have to be perfect either! Your Transformational Purpose Statement will continue to evolve over time.

2. **Be Brief:** Try to write a single sentence that contains 25 words or less. It must be something you can internalize and memorize, especially when you're in the heat of a coaching moment.

3. **Be Deliberate:** Be precise with the words and topics you choose. What relationships matter to you the most? What is the outcome you desire to see?

4. **Be Structured:** Think verb-target-outcome. The verb describes how you most successfully interact with people according to your gifting (see Identifying Your Gifting). The target is the audience or relationships you aim to impact. The outcome is the transformational cause you are pursuing and should incorporate your highest core values.

Identifying Your Gifting: What verbs listed below best describe how you most successfully interact with people? Use these verbs or write your own in the blank spaces to craft your Transformational Purpose Statement.

Act	Coach	Construct	Create
Demonstrate	Develop	Educate	Empower
Encourage	Help	Identify	Initiate
Inspire	Lead	Love	Manage
Mentor	Model	Motivate	Plan
Prepare	Produce	Recognize	Relate
Fuel	Study	Teach	Tell
_____	_____	_____	_____

Sample Transformational Purpose Statement:
"To **inspire** (verb) **coaches** and **athletes** (target) toward the **pursuit of excellence** in sports and life while **enjoying the journey** (outcome)."

My Transformational Purpose Statement is:

_____

_____

_____

_____

_____

ABOUT FCA

Since 1954, FCA has challenged coaches and athletes at every level to use the powerful platform of sport to reach every coach and athlete with the transforming power of Jesus Christ. FCA serves local communities in over 100 countries, seeking to Engage, Equip and Empower coaches and athletes to make disciples who make disciples.

VISION
To see the world transformed by Jesus Christ through the influence of coaches and athletes.

MISSION
To lead every coach and athlete into a growing relationship with Jesus Christ and His church.

VALUES
Integrity, Serving, Teamwork, Excellence

For general questions on FCA and how to find local FCA staff, visit www.FCA.org or call 1-800-289-0909.

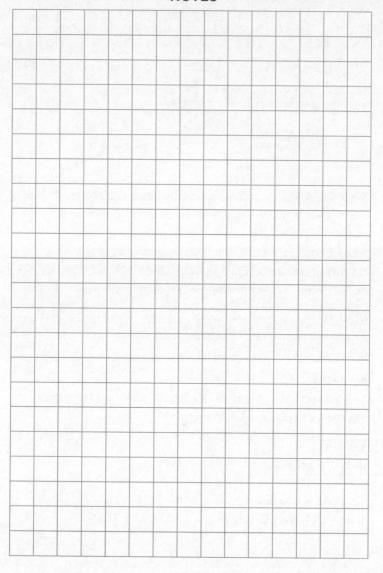